SEEING THROUGH NEW EYES

Using the PAWN Process in Faith-Based Groups

A Renewal Enterprise, Inc.

Chicago

Other books in The Renewable Organization™ Series:

The Future Starts Now: The Renewable Organization™ for Faith-Based Groups

Do What Matters: The 4-D Cycle™ for Faith-Based Groups

The Renewable Practices™ Series for Faith-Based Groups

- *19 (or more) Ideas for Asking Purposeful Questions*
- *19 (or more) Ideas for Using Participative Processes*
- *19 (or more) Ideas for Working Playfully*
- *19 (or more) Ideas for Taking Place Seriously*
- *19 (or more) Ideas for Being Reproductive*
- *19 (or more) Ideas for Seeing Possibilities*
- *19 (or more) Ideas for Igniting Passion*

Other books by the authors of *Seeing Through New Eyes: Using the PAWN Process in Faith-Based Groups.*

Fryer, K. **Dancing Down the Hallway: Spiritual Reflections for the Everyday**. Augsburg Fortress, 2001.

Fryer, K. **Reclaiming the "L" Word: Renewing the Church from its Lutheran Core**. Augsburg Fortress, 2003.

Fryer, K., Dave Daubert. **A Story Worth Sharing: Engaging Evangelism**. Minneapolis: Augsburg Fortress, 2004.

Fryer, K. **No Experience Necessary: 8 Unit Bible Study**. Minneapolis: Augsburg Fortress, 2005.

Fryer, K. **Reclaiming the "C" Word: Daring to Be Church Again**. Minneapolis: Augsburg Fortress, 2006.

Daubert, D. **Living Lutheran: Renewing Your Congregation**. Minneapolis: Augsburg Fortress, 2007.

Fryer, K. **No Experience Necessary. Everybody's Welcome**. Revised and expanded. Minneapolis: Augsburg Fortress, 2007.

Fryer, K. **Reclaiming the "E" Word: Waking Up to Our Evangelical Identity**. Minneapolis: Augsburg Fortress, 2008.

Daubert, D., Tana Kjos. **Reclaiming the "V" Word: Renewing Life At Its Vocational Core** Minneapolis: Augsburg Fortress, 2009.

Visit the A.R.E. blog at www.arenewalenterprise.com for a ton of free articles and to learn more about how you can put the principles, practices and processes of a Renewable Organization™ to work in your faith community, congregation, judicatory, denomination, faith-based school or agency.

Published by A Renewal Enterprise, Inc.
Copyright © A Renewal Enterprise, Inc., 2010

All rights reserved under International and Pan-American Copyright Conventions. No part of this book may be reproduced in any form or by any electronic or mechanical means, including information storage and retrieval systems, without permission in writing from the publisher, except by a reviewer, who may quote brief passages in a review. Published in 2010 by ARE Books, a division of A Renewal Enterprise, Ltd. Distributed by A Renewal Enterprise, Inc., Chicago.

www.arenewalenterprise.com

Includes bibliographic references.

ISBN 978-0-9842356-1-2

Contributors:

Marlene Daubert
Tana Kjos
Robert Machamer
Catherine Pate
Jennifer Lee Robinson

Layout and Design: Instant Noodles Design
Production Editor: Catherine Pate
Scribes: Dave Daubert and Kelly A. Fryer

Printed and bound in the United States of America.
This book is printed on recycled acid-free paper that meets the minimum requirements American National Standard Institute Z39.48 (Permanence of Paper).

For every teacher along the way who helped us see.

CONTENTS

INTRODUCTION

> *"Jesus is calling us, jut as we are—*
> *with no more than the clothes*
> *on our backs—to jump on board*
> *and be a part of what God is up*
> *to in the world."*

Jesus said "For, in fact, the kingdom of God is among you."
(Luke 17:21b)

Jesus has a present tense mindset. Throughout his ministry on earth, he spent much of his time and energy trying to help people see the kingdom of God right where they were.

Today, God is on the loose in the world! God is blessing, healing, feeding, reconciling, forgiving, loving, creating and setting people free *right now*. You are invited to be a part of that work.

Without a doubt, you and the organization you care about will be and are being transformed in many and marvelous ways as you answer Jesus' call to participate in God's work in the world. But you don't need to be someone or something other than who you are, right now, in order to answer that call. You also don't need to sit on the sidelines, waiting until you know enough or have enough of whatever it is you think you're lacking to do something that makes a difference. Jesus is calling us, just as we are—with nothing more than the clothes on our backs—to jump on board and be a part of what God is up to in the world.

It all comes down to three basic principles that we learn from Jesus (Matthew 4:17-22). We call them the principles of a Renewable Organization™. They are behind all of the work we're doing at A Renewal Enterprise, Inc. these days:

- **Be who you are;**
- **See what you have;**
- **Do what matters.**

Together, our team is learning what it means to live out these principles in our own lives, and we're working hard to help others learn them, too.

The process strategies and leadership practices that we're teaching are not designed to help you get to some 'preferred future.' We don't think it's worth time or energy to paint a picture of what your ministry or context *might* look like a hundred years down the road. And we won't promise that if you adopt these principles your ministry will survive for the next hundred—or even a dozen—years. Don't believe anyone who does. But we do think it's possible to catch a glimpse of what God is doing right now in your context that you can be a part of, and we think that's what really matters.

One of the resources we've developed to help people and the organizations they care about *be who they are and see what they have for the sake of doing what matters* is called the PAWN process. This simple but radical process strategy can help you see what is emerging in your context.

We have used the PAWN process to help organizations like yours develop an umbrella strategy (i.e., purpose, principles and strategic directions). It can be useful whenever you have a big decision to make or when it's time to set a new course in your work together. But we believe, more importantly, that the PAWN process can help open your eyes to what God is up to every single day so that you can jump in and be a part of it.

We have been deeply influenced in the development of this process by research being done in the growing field of social innovation.

Places like Social Innovation Generation at the University of Waterloo, Ontario, and the Center for Social Innovation at Stanford University are leading the way in inspiring and educating leaders to champion and work for transformative social change.

You will also see traces of design thinking in our work. But the PAWN process has, above all, emerged from our work as theologians and leaders in faith-based organizations.

Here we defer to sources like Tim Brown who wrote a very insightful book, *Change by Design: How Design Thinking Transforms Organizations and Inspires Innovation.*

This book explores how you can use the PAWN process to see what is emerging in your faith community or faith-based organization. Chapter One describes some of the theological and theoretical ideas behind this process strategy. Chapter Two gives you an overview of the PAWN process. Chapters Three, Four and Five will help you understand and use each of the three PAWN lenses. Chapter Six will help you bring it all together and begin using the PAWN process in a way that is dynamic and ongoing.

The kingdom is among us. It is here. Right now. See?

CHAPTER ONE:
A NEW WAY OF SEEING

"Everybody involved had the best of intentions. The problem is that none of the outreach team members knew anything about how to pull off a pet blessing. As a matter of fact, none of them even owned a pet."

The pastor of a small congregation in a mid-size town in Ontario called us on the phone one sunny afternoon to say, "I get it!" Outreach team members in her congregation had spent months banging their heads against the wall, trying to check off one more thing on their strategic plans for the year. They were supposed to be planning a pet blessing because the leaders who wrote the plan had discovered that a lot of people in town had pets, and they thought blessing those pets would be a good outreach event. They were even going to do the pet blessing right on the front lawn of the courthouse to get as much exposure as possible. Everybody involved had the best of intentions. The problem was that none of the outreach team members knew anything about how to pull off a pet blessing. As a matter of fact, none of them even owned a pet.

> The blessing of pets takes place most often on or near October 4 to commemorate the Feast Day of Saint Francis of Assisi (the patron saint of animals). Incidentally, you can actually Google instructions on how to hold and attend a pet blessing.

The pastor, who does happen to be a pet owner, was telling this story to her vet one day. He didn't ask why a bunch of people without pets would try to plan a pet blessing, but he did wonder why they would have it at the courthouse. "Why not do it at the dog park?" he asked. The pastor got very excited about that idea. The dog park has a built-in audience! No planning required! Just show up with a sprinkler and let the blessing begin! Her vet said she might want to contain her enthusiasm long enough to phone up the chairperson of the dog park board. You know, just to ask if it'd be OK.

The dog park board couldn't have been more excited. Before you knew it, they were volunteering to do all the advertising. They even got the pet stores in town to donate doggie-bags full of treats for all the pet blessing participants.

The chamber of commerce offered to cook up and give away hot dogs to the pet owners. An ice cream shop gave away free goodies to the kids who came. What about the outreach team? They helped wherever and however they were needed.

Hundreds of people gathered together for a hot-dog-and-ice-cream-fueled good time. Pets by the dozens, together with their owners, stood under a blue sky and received the Lord's blessing. New friends were made. A community was blessed. And people knew something holy happened that day at the dog park.

DO YOU GET IT?

What our friend, the pet-blessing-pastor, 'got' is how life-giving it is to be set free from your own agenda so that you can let yourself get caught up in God's agenda; to give up the idea of control so that you can follow where the Spirit leads; to quit beating your head against the wall of your own organization so that you can get involved in what God is up to in the world.

It might sound strange for us to say but, in our experience, being a part of what God is up to in the world is the last thing most faith-based organizations (yes, even congregations!) have been doing. Lots of them have been doing things *for* God, *in the name of* God, or because they think they're following God's command. But they haven't actually been *joining* in the things God is already doing. There are a lot of reasons for this. But, trust us: everything changes once you realize that God really is on the loose in the world, at work in your context, doing things in and through both you and your neighbors.

Once you get that, suddenly you're no longer killing yourself trying to make ministry happen. You're not sitting around dreaming up big plans of what you might do one day if and when you find the right people, have enough money or decide to finally get around to it.

You're also no longer feeling sorry for yourself because you don't have the resources to do whatever it is you think you're supposed to do, the things you used to be able to do, or the things your competitor down the street is doing. You're just paying attention—getting to know your neighbors, probing the passions and uncovering the gifts of people in your organization, asking good questions, exploring possibilities, keeping your eyes open for the things around you that are making God smile, daring to see the things that are breaking God's heart. And, when you sense a movement of the Spirit creating some new opportunity or leading you in a surprising new direction, you're joining in to help.

This way of seeing is one of the keys to living and working in renewable ways. It is how the most resilient, adaptable and effective ministries will function in the emerging future.

WHAT'S THE MOST EXCITING THING THAT HAS HAPPENED IN YOUR WORK LATELY?

Just for fun, draw a picture of it right here.

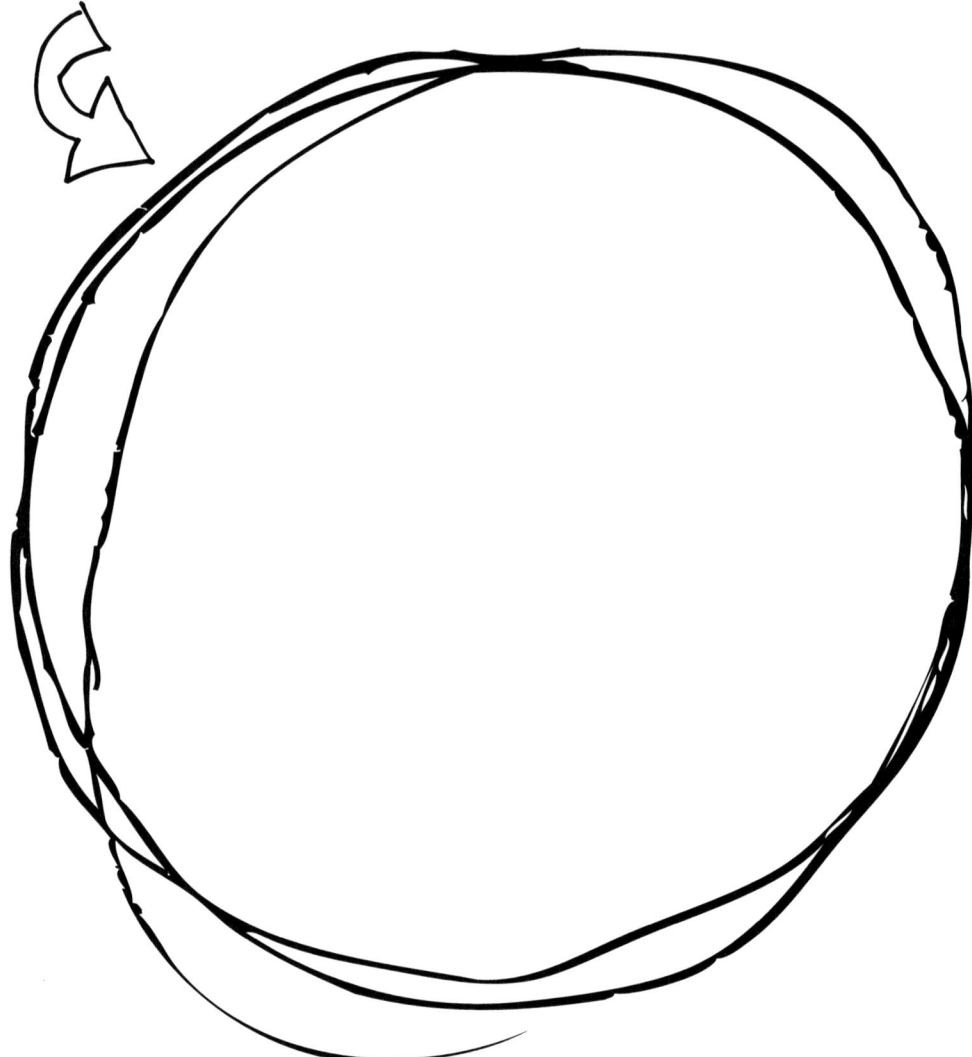

Now, think about how it all happened: How much of it did you actually plan? How much of it seemed to just 'happen'?

AN ACT TO FOLLOW

In our experience, most of the exciting things that happen in life and work aren't carefully planned out ahead of time. Neither do they just spontaneously occur. Rather, they happen because we have done two things at the same time. We have dared to set a course and take action, and we have simultaneously stayed open to the surprising things that emerged along the way.

There is some very exciting research being done these days in the field of social innovation that confirms our experience. Social science researchers who are studying how transformation happens in complex systems will tell you about the importance of intentionality; leaders have to commit to doing something. But these researchers will also tell you about the role of *emergence,* a concept they are borrowing from the natural sciences to describe the unpredictable things that happen because of the interaction between elements, but which appear to be outside of anyone's control. In other words, they'll tell you that nothing will happen unless you decide to do something, but no matter what you do, the outcome isn't ultimately going to be up to you.[1]

That's pretty much what the earliest Christians discovered, too. The book of Acts opens as Jesus is giving them final instructions, "...you will receive power when the Holy Spirit has come upon you; and you will be my witnesses in Jerusalem, in all Judea and Samaria, and to the ends of the earth." (Acts 1:8). It wasn't a lot, but it was enough. Jesus' followers walked away with a sense of direction and began a journey together that would lead them places they never could have imagined.

[1] Francis Westley, et al, *Getting To Maybe,* 2006.

Although those early Christians kick-started what is arguably the most influential movement in history, they'd be the first to say that they didn't make anything happen. They believed the Spirit was at work in, through and all around them—and when they saw the Spirit at work they joined in. They told the man with bum legs to get up and walk, they climbed into a stranger's chariot, they sang until their prison walls came tumbling down, they baptized Gentiles and they put women in charge.

None of these things would have happened if those guys hadn't been willing to move out and follow the course Jesus had given them. They did have to do something. But they didn't really *plan* anything that happened along the way. In fact, when they tried to carefully plan something, it didn't work out so well. Just ask Mathias. He's the only disciple who was chosen using anything resembling a plan. The other disciples, caught up by the idea of replacing the traitor Judas, actually developed a list of job qualifications! And Mathias met them (Acts 1:15-26).

Unfortunately, we don't know much more than that about him; he disappears from the story and is never heard from again.

Make a list of all the great dramas in the biblical story.
Go ahead, we'll wait:
Example: Moses leading the Hebrews out of slavery.

_____

_____

_____

_____

_____

How much of what happened in each of these stories did somebody (besides God) actually plan out ahead of time? How much of it happened because somebody in the story was paying attention to what God was doing and dared to join in?

See. We told you so.

A DIRECT CHALLENGE

The most effective leaders in the emerging future—the ones who create purposeful, resilient, adaptable movements and organizations—will be those leaders who recognize both the importance, and the limitations of planning. They will understand that they are called to a journey, not a destination, and that along the way they can expect to be surprised by paths, people and possibilities they never imagined. They will relinquish the idea of control, and replace it with a commitment to participate in what God is up to.

Relinquishing the idea that you can control the outcome of your life and work through careful planning and execution is a real challenge for most people, even faith-based leaders. That's because this approach is anathema to the organizational model that virtually all organizations, including faith-based ones in most of North America, are using today.

It is a direct challenge to *the way we've always done things*, at least since the dawn of the industrial era.

Problem Alert

Throughout the nineteenth and twentieth centuries, titans of industry like Henry Ford built complex systems and accomplished remarkable levels of productivity and efficiency, delivering more products to more markets with greater speed than ever before. Management learned to adopt a command and control approach and bureaucracy swelled to meet the need of rapidly expanding social systems. The achievements of this period were, in fact, revolutionary. But they were not without their downside. These factories burned up and guzzled down the earth's natural resources, and they used people like they were disposable too. People became little more than cogs in these elaborate machines.

Behind this modern organizational model is a supporting narrative that teaches you to see the world as a threat to your organization. In this world of scarce consumable resources, according to the story, you are in competition for your survival. If you don't plan carefully and execute that plan efficiently, you risk failing to acquire the consumables you and your organization need; your competitor will win them instead; and you will die.

Some academic and business leaders believe we are witnessing the beginning of the end of this era right now. As one industry after another teeters on the brink of bankruptcy, the consumptive foundation of this system is rotting beneath it, sucking the life out of people and wrecking the planet.

A host of cross-disciplinary voices are calling for a new way of living and working together. It's especially ironic to us, therefore, that the consumable approach to life and work continues to dominate the way ministry is done in North America.

For many Christians across the denominational spectrum, the unfortunate narrative behind the consumable approach that characterizes the modern industrial era is strengthened by a theology that takes a similarly dim view of the world. In other words, in most faith-based organizations today, an organizational theory that sees the world as a threat is working hand in hand with a theology that sees it that way, too. Although God might love the world, in this theological narrative, it isn't a place you are encouraged to look for God's activity. It is, instead, something that needs to be converted or fixed. It is the object of your evangelical and/or justice-making efforts. It has to be saved and it's your job (with the Spirit's help) to do it. In fact, each Sunday morning you are most likely 'sent' back out into the world, not to be on the lookout for what God is already doing, but to serve the Lord who sends you by doing good works for needy people, telling the good news to desperate people and hopefully bringing a pew-full of new members back with you the next time you come.

This theological narrative has different variations depending on whether it's being told in the mainline, evangelical, missional and/or emerging churches. In every case, however, the inevitable result is a consumable approach to ministry that objectifies the world and turns our neighbors (and their money) into consumers or consumable resources that churches and other faith-based organizations compete with each other to win. These narratives are deeply engrained in most church leaders. We confess that we bought into them ourselves for many years. It's the way the story was passed down to us.

In fact, confession is as good a place as any to begin making the necessary shift. It's helpful to acknowledge that both our theology and our life together have been in bondage to the consumable approach of the modern industrial era. It's healthy to repent of the desire to control our own destiny (and every detail of next week's annual campaign kickoff dinner) and the fear that drove us to it. We thought we were fighting for our survival after all.

Making the shift to a new, renewable way of living and working together will not be easy. We're not fooling ourselves about this. You shouldn't either.

OK, we're forgiven. Now what?

A RENEWABLE WAY OF WORKING

The alternative to a consumable way of life is a renewable one. In a consumable approach, your whole focus is on survival in the midst of a threatening environment. All of your energy is devoted to getting the scarce resources (e.g., money, people) you need to survive. Consequently, these resources are viewed as disposable—objects to be recruited or consumed for the survival of the institution.

Because organizational perpetuation dominates all other concerns, leaders are easily trapped by self-centered, life-sucking and unsustainable ways of working. They often over plan, micromanage and make unreasonable demands on their co-workers, their subordinates and themselves. People who find themselves being treated as a resource (often in subliminal ways) burn out. A sense of purposelessness pervades your life together, eventually causing people to feel overwhelmed by a sense of scarcity, finitude and fear.

In a renewable approach, the primary focus isn't institutional survival. The bottom line is *doing what matters*—making a positive difference to people, to the organization you care about and to the planet.

For faith-based leaders, doing what matters means participating in the work God is doing in the world—bringing reconciliation, healing and blessings. The world is viewed as the locus of God's loving activity, rather than something to be used up and thrown away. Everything God has made is honored as valuable; people are seen as treasures in clay jars.

When individuals are encouraged to bring all of their gifts and passions to your shared work, your organization becomes more creative and adaptable. Set free from the defensiveness of protecting an organization from running out of resources, people are more willing to risk trying new things. Aware of God's abundant Spirit, leaders work with a generous spirit that is other-focused, life-giving and sustainable. People feel useful rather than used up. A sense of deep joy pervades your life together, making your organization resilient even in the most difficult circumstances.

Making the shift from a consumable to a renewable way of working isn't about learning a bunch of new tactics. It requires a completely different worldview; a transformation in the way you think as much as in the way you see and do things. This shift begins when you make these three commitments:

COMMITMENT #1
DECIDE TO DO WHAT MATTERS

The shift from a consumable to a renewable way of living and working together begins when you decide to do what matters. You cannot serve two bottom lines: God's agenda and your institutional survival. Why not? Jesus said so, "No one can serve two masters; for a slave will either hate the one and love the other, or be devoted to the one and despise the other. You cannot serve God and wealth." (Matthew 6:24). You pick.

God is up to something much bigger and more important than the survival of the institutions we care about. God is on the loose in the world *right now*, inviting us to participate in a loving mission to reconcile the whole creation and set all people free. What could possibly matter more than that?

Think about the people Jesus was most irritated by. Many were overly religious and not particularly concerned about being useful to God in the world. They thought that simply being religious, especially if they were in charge, was enough. It irritated Jesus to no end when people acted like the whole point of religion was...religion.

God's primary concerns then, as now, are the people and planet that God has made. Jesus saw overly-pious, inwardly-focused, ritually-obsessed religious leaders as dangerous because they not only distracted people from what God is up to in the world, they were often a barrier for people who wanted to get involved. Religion that is in the way of what God is up to in the world—no matter how impressive it smells, sounds or looks—is a waste of the gifts God has given, and Jesus wants nothing to do with it.

Decide to do what matters. Choose God's agenda ahead of your own. Commit to doing life and work in a way that is useful to God.

COMMITMENT #2
KEEP YOUR EYES OPEN

Another group of people Jesus was frequently irritatated with were people who watched God do something and simply couldn't see it. For example, think about the story from Mark's gospel when Jesus started warning his disciples about "the yeast of the Pharisees." His point was that all the Pharisees cared about was religion (see above). But the disciples were so hungry and so preoccupied by the fact that they forgot to bring lunch with them that they missed the point. All they could think about was *yeast=bread*. And they were worried about not having any. Never mind that they had just seen Jesus feed 10,000 people (5,000 men plus all the women and children), heal sick people and cast out demons. They didn't get it. *How many miracles do I have to do before you guys stop worrying about having enough to eat?!* Jesus must have thought. Frustrated, he said, "Do you have eyes, and fail to see? Do you have ears, and fail to hear? And do you not remember?" (Mark 8:18) In other words, *guys, God is on the loose! God's work has been unfolding right in front of you. Did you see any of it? Or did you seriously miss the whole thing?*

God is on the loose and at work in the world right now. Your environment is not a threat to be managed, fixed, converted or saved. It is the locus of God's activity. God is up to something in your life, in the organization you care about, in your community. Pay attention. The PAWN process can help. But you have to decide to keep your eyes open, believing there is something out there to see.

COMMITMENT #3
GO WITH THE FLOW

Wrap your head around the idea that you are being called to do what matters to God but you have no control over the outcome, and there is no way to predict where this journey will take you. We know this is going to be a hard one, especially for you Type A personalities out there. It might help to spend a little time reflecting on these Proverbs: (Take as much time as you need.)

"The human mind plans the way, but the LORD directs the steps." (16:9)

"Sometimes there is a way that seems to be right, but in the end it is the way to death." (16:25)

"Before destruction one's heart is haughty, but humility goes before honor." (18:12)

"The human mind may devise many plans, but it is the purpose of the LORD that will be established." (19:21)

"Do not boast about tomorrow, for you do not know what a day may bring." (27:1)

Here's the deal: Don't waste your time making elaborate plans. Quit trying to predict (or control!) the future. Stop measuring "progress" by how many consumable resources (e.g., butts and bucks) you pull in. It's sucking the life out of you and the people you're working with. Effective leaders in the emerging future will invest their time and energy in discerning God's direction. And they'll learn to go with the flow. What's flow? You'll know it when you feel it.

The pastor of a suburban congregation in the eastern part of the U.S. emailed to tell us that after hearing one of our presentations she just "tried doing a few of the things" we talked about in her circles of influence. In response, she started with her congregational council (like a board of directors). And then she hosted a couple of "leadership summits." She invited anybody who "looked like a leader," but opened it up to whoever wanted to attend. We don't know exactly what happened at these events, but she says they generated a lot of good energy and conversation; and then things started to happen. She did her best to encourage people. She said "yes!" a lot. But mostly she has just tried to stay out of the way and not squash things as they emerged.

One woman who "caught some of the energy of leading with purpose for the sake of those who are on the journey with her" started a small group that is, among other things, learning how to play together. One week they were studying the story about Jesus embracing the children. "We have a very active nursery school in the building," the pastor reported, "so [this woman] arranged for the group to spend 1/2 hour in the classrooms observing (and playing) with the kids. Then the nursery school director came to them and they all talked about being a child and how a child learns. Now they have an adult play day (when they get to play with the kids' toys) scheduled." Just imagine how differently those adults will lead, having learned how to play together.

A book group in the same congregation was reading Jodi Piccoult's *My Sister's Keeper*. They realized they didn't really know how to talk about bioethics. One member suggested they try learning from their neighbors. They invited a local man from the community who is knowledgeable about these issues to come talk with them; he agreed to come the next week. Another member of the group, who also studies at the synagogue in town, called a member there to learn about a Jewish perspective on bioethics "and the next thing we knew, he was with us one Sunday to talk about it." Just picture the new possibilities that may emerge as the people in these congregations develop relationships with one another and begin to pay closer attention to the places where their passions and interests converge. Our pastor friend has another leadership summit planned. "[We are] moving ahead," she wrote, "into the unknown!"

CHAPTER TWO
AN OVERVIEW OF THE PAWN PROCESS

"The PAWN process can train you to recognize what can be so difficult to see."

A friend of ours recently attended a workshop at his job. Like a lot of workshops these days, the presenter was using an LCD projector to show slides throughout the day. On one slide he showed the image that is on the next page and asked a simple question, "What do you see?" We're asking you the same question. (Turn the page now).

"What do you see?" the workshop leader asked. "A dot," replied everyone in the group. "Are you sure?" he checked. "Yes," they said again, "a dot."

What do *you* see?

_____

_____

_____

_____

_____

_____

_____

_____

The presenter shared that studies show that over ninety-nine percent of people who see the previous page projected on a screen see only a black dot. Even though less than one percent of the screen is black and ninety-nine percent of the screen is white, virtually no one articulates seeing the white space on the screen. It is almost invisible to them. Our eyes have been trained to filter things out to see what is perceived as the most important, which means our eyes block out most of what we actually see.

This exercise is a variation on the age-old question about whether the glass is half full or half empty. The optimist sees a glass half full of water—the pessimist sees a glass half empty. While both are focused on the water, neither notices the air. And although most people don't think about it, what's the most important thing in the glass, at least in the short term? The air, of course. Within minutes you would die without it.

Both of these examples illustrate the way in which the questions we ask and the assumptions we bring determine what we are able to see. Seeing with new eyes is about retraining ourselves to notice things we have been trained to miss. It's about raising new questions and daring to challenge our assumptions. It's about paying attention to things that have always been there, but we have been conditioned not to notice.

The PAWN process is a strategy to help you practice seeing what you might otherwise have missed. Anyone can use it, in any situation. It helps you see what *is* and what *is emerging* in your context.

But for Christians, the PAWN process is a unique way of paying attention to what God is up to in the world so that you can name it and jump in to be a part of it all. This process requires a lot of discipline at first in order to retrain your eyes to see what you may not have seen so well, but over time it will become natural. You will find yourself noticing things you never knew were there, and you'll be surprised by all of the possibilities for action that are emerging right before your very eyes.

WHAT MAKES IT SO HARD TO SEE GOD'S ACTIVITY?

The world is not an object to be conquered or a resource to be consumed. The biblical story tells us the world is actually the locus of God's activity. God is at work 'out there,' inviting everyone to join in the work of co-creation, bringing healing and freedom to all, right now.

We're not going to hold it against you if you struggle to see evidence of God's activity in the world. There are all kinds of reasons why that might be difficult. The way the Bible tells it, most people missed it even when God was actually down here walking around two thousand years ago.

List some of the reasons it might have been hard for people who met Jesus back then to realize they were seeing God at work:

_____

_____

_____

_____

_____

_____

_____

_____

_____

_____

_____

_____

_____

Why is it sometimes hard for people to recognize God's activity in the world today?

_____

_____

_____

_____

_____

_____

Which of the things on that list do you struggle with the most?

_____

_____

_____

_____

_____

_____

One good reason people are hesitant to say what they think God is doing in the world is that they know they might be...well...wrong. And it would be wrong to say that you could ever know, without question or hesitation, what God is up to. It could even be dangerous. Don't even ask the question unless you're prepared to hear something you don't want to hear. Don't ask it without being willing to test what you're hearing next to, and even against both the biblical story and what others are hearing. And don't ask it unless you're willing to admit that you can't possibly get more than a glimpse of what God is doing in the world.

You have been created to participate in God's mission to bring in a kingdom of peace and reconciliation. It is possible to get a glimpse of what that looks like in your context so that you can be a part of it.

THIS WILL TAKE PRACTICE

The PAWN process can train you to recognize what can be so difficult to see. It can help you see what is and the possibilities for action that are emerging in your context.

It can help Christians pay attention to what God is up to in their own lives, in their faith communities, and in their neighborhood. But, at first, using this process strategy may make you feel like a newborn child trying to get things into focus.

For people with relatively normal vision, seeing is an almost effortless process. Yet anyone who has watched a baby in the weeks after it is born knows that it doesn't just happen. Newborn eyes struggle to find focus, failing most of the time for a while. Over time, the two eyes and the brain learn to work together. Because the lens in each eye is a single lens, everything that goes through it is focused and inverts as it passes through the eye. When the brain gets the image, it is actually upside down. Not only that but, because there are two eyes, there are two images. Each lens provides a similar but slightly different perspective on the scene outside. The brain has to learn to align its understanding of what is coming in from these two images into a single picture. And it has to imagine both of them right side up. Although some people never fully get this process to function smoothly, most people master it during the first few months of life. As long as it functions well, they never notice again. They see in a seemingly simple and almost effortless process.

Similarly, trying to see what God is up to using the PAWN process will take work at first. It will take time and practice. Eventually, you won't need to be conscious of the PAWN process to pay attention to God's activity. You will be on the lookout for it, naturally.

We've tried to diagram the PAWN process to make it a little easier for you to practice seeing with new eyes. But it's frustrating to do this in a two-dimensional format. Drawn on paper this way, even we know it looks static. It appears that each of these "lenses" is meant to be used in lock-step order. They're not. When you look at this diagram, try to imagine everything moving at once. Try to imagine seeing through each of these lenses at the same time. Imagine overlapping spaces instead of "sequential steps."[2]

---

[2] This is language used by Tim Brown, CEO of the design firm IDEO and author of *Change By Design* (2009).

The PAWN Process™
Practicing a renewable way of seeing

**Lens #1:
Your Purpose**
"Raison d'être" – your
reason for being

DISCOVER!
**Visions for
Action Emerge**

**Lens #2:
Your Neighbor/Context**
A) **A**ssets, gifts and passions
B) **W**ow! Good things already happening
C) **N**eeds of your neighbors

Lens #3: You
A) **A**ssets, gifts and passions
B) **W**ow! Good things already happening
C) **N**eeds in your life/organization

THREE LENSES

Notice that there are four arrows in the PAWN process diagram.
Three of these arrows point inward and each represents a
different "lens," all of which together produce a clearer vision
of what is happening and what is possible in your context right
now.

All three lenses are necessary. Just as your brain needs
more than one lens (hence, you have two eyes) to bring things

into full perspective and achieve a clear sense of depth and distance, each of these lenses contributes something to the whole picture. By itself, each lens brings accurate information about some aspect of what is happening in your context. But, by itself, each lens also brings a limited perspective; it lacks fullness and depth without the others.

You might also notice, if you look carefully, that there isn't any part of this process that makes it uniquely "Christian." And you don't have to be a Christian (or a person with any faith at all) to use it to help you see what is and what is emerging in your context. It can help you—whoever you are—see what you have for the sake of doing what matters to you, to the organization you care about and to the world we all share.

But Christians will quickly recognize that each of the lenses in the PAWN process is connected to the great commandment of Jesus. That's why we can use it to catch a vibrant glimpse into the dynamic work of God in this world—work in which we, God and our neighbors are all engaged in meaningful ways.

The gospel writer, Matthew, tells us that Jesus was teaching publicly and being tested by some leaders who disliked his work. One of the leaders, wanting to trap Jesus publicly, asked him, "Which is the greatest commandment?" Jesus replied, "'You shall love the Lord your God with all your heart, and with all your soul, and with all your mind.' This is the greatest and first commandment. And a second is like it: 'You shall love your neighbor as yourself.' On these two commandments hang all the law and the prophets.'" (Matt 22:37-40).

Jesus understood life is lived most fully when people love God, other people and themselves. When you, God and your neighbor are all well-connected and interrelated, life is as it should be. When any of these connections breaks down, whether between you and God or between you and your neighbor, then things fall short of what God intends. The PAWN process honors Jesus' commandment by reminding you that it is God's intention that you, your neighbor and God work together, in healthy, meaningful and productive ways, on the things that matter to God.

WHY "PAWN?"

It's helpful to be reminded that, like the pawn on a chess board, each one of us is called to be on the front lines of God's mission in the world. From the very beginning, God has called people to participate in the work of creation. God is blessing, reconciling, healing, loving, freeing and bringing peace in the world. The whole point of our lives is to be a part of that adventure. There is no other purpose for our lives than that one.

PAWN is also an acronym. Each letter in PAWN stands for something:

(P) Purpose: This is our reason for being. It is why we exist. As Christians, we believe that our purpose is connected to God's mission in the world. God is up to something and our purpose helps us stay clear about the part we play.

(A) Assets, Gifts and Passions: These are the resources we have to help us fulfill our purpose. We believe these are gifts from God and that they are given both to us and to our neighbors.

(W) Wows!: These are the good things already happening that we can leverage to fulfill our purpose. You might say these are the things that are making God smile in your life, in the organization you care about and in your context.

(N) Needs: These are the needs or issues that must be addressed and/or resourced in order for us to fulfill our purpose. You might say these are the things that are breaking God's heart. Sometimes these things provide the impetus or drive we need to do what we're being called to do.

Notice that each of these four components is organized into the three lenses—your purpose, neighbor, you—of the PAWN process.

Lens #1:
Your Purpose
"Raison d'être" – your reason for being

Lens #2:
Your Neighbor/Context
A) **A**ssets, gifts and passions
B) **W**ow! Good things already happening
C) **N**eeds of your neighbors

Lens #3: You
A) **A**ssets, gifts and passions
B) **W**ow! Good things already happening
C) **N**eeds in your life/organization

What else do you notice about the PAWN process?

What questions are developing for you?

> *What are you getting excited about as you think about learning to see with new eyes?*

THE GREAT SURPRISE

Refer back to the PAWN process illustration on page 43. Notice that the three arrows representing each of the three lenses (purpose, neighbor, you) all point to a central eye. That's because they work together to produce vision. But this is NOT a vision of the future you are going to pursue and build. When the three lenses of the PAWN process converge, they give you a vision of what is already happening right now and the new possibilities that are emerging in your midst.

So many organizations today, including faith-based ones, are starved for something they think and hope and pray might work. They are trapped in the "if-only" thinking that characterizes the modern consumable approach to life and work, and they have grown accustomed to using *The Great Excuse* (see page 94). By using the three lenses of the PAWN process, they will suddenly be surprised by the many possibilities and doable options that emerge from seeing what God is already up to in the world right now.

As you explore each of the lenses in the PAWN process, the goal is not to see far into the future and then try to produce long-term goals and action plans. Rather, the PAWN process invites you to see a vision that is emerging from within your context right now as you go with the flow, joining God and your neighbors in *doing what matters.*

CHAPTER THREE
THE SENSE-MAKING LENS

"In many faith-based organizations, people assume they have a shared sense of purpose that they don't really have and it's been a long time since they talked about it together."

Our parents, living here in North America, remember being afraid of polio. They knew kids who got it. They saw how it crippled its victims. They knew it could kill you. Nothing else in history has caused more cases of disability than this fast-acting virus. As recently as 1985, there were 350,000 cases of polio reported somewhere in the world, most of which struck children under the age of five. Today, polio has been all but eradicated.[3] The work of Rotary International is one of the primary reasons for this.

One of the most successful civic grassroots organizations in the world, Rotary International, which was founded in 1905 in Chicago, Illinois, has grown to become a worldwide organization with 1.2 million Rotarians belonging to 32,000 clubs in more than 200 countries and geographical areas.

One reason for their incredible success is that they are very clear about their purpose. They know who they are and what matters to them. Guided by the motto, "Service above self," the primary focus of the organization is clear—service—and they encourage their members to live personal lives of service as well.

With their purpose clearly in view, Rotary International has developed a handful of concise strategic directions that make it possible for them to focus their resources in a way that really makes a difference:

- *Combat hunger*
- *Improve health and sanitation*
- *Provide education and job training*
- *Promote peace*
- *Eradicate polio*

Are you and your organization this clear about who you are and what you are about?

[3] These facts about polio are from the website of Rotary International. http://www.rotary.org/en/ServiceAndFellowship/Polio/FactsAboutPolio/Pages/ridefault.aspx

UNDER THE UMBRELLA

For faith-based leaders, the PAWN process combines three lenses to help you keep your eyes open for what God is up to so that you can join in and do what matters.

The first of these three lenses helps you maintain clarity about who you are and what you are about so that as things emerge in your context you have a sense of what your role in it all might be. In this way, it is what you might call the sense-making lens. Without it, the other two lenses would help you see what God is up to inside your organization and in your community, but it would just look like a jumble of activity; you wouldn't have any idea what your role in all of it is supposed to be or how you can be useful to God.

This first lens helps you make sense of what you're seeing by keeping you focused on what God's fundamental purpose and direction is for you and your organization. It represents the "P" (i.e., purpose) in the PAWN acronym, but it actually includes three critical components:

Lens #1: Your Purpose "Raison d'être" – your reason for being

- *A sense of purpose*
- *A set of guiding principles*
- *A set of strategic directions*

Together, these three components—purpose, guiding principles and strategic directions—provide an *umbrella strategy* for your organization's work.

An umbrella strategy is very different from a traditional

strategic plan, which typically the top leaders in an organization develop to answer questions like: *What do we do? Who is our target audience? How are we going to beat the competition?* These plans can feel like a straitjacket to the people stuck having to carry them out, especially in a rapidly changing context when their jobs depend on meeting their goals.

An umbrella strategy, on the other hand, is most effective when it has been discerned and articulated using radically participative processes that get everybody in your organization involved. It answers questions like: *Who are we? What really matters? Where can we focus our resources in a way that will really make a difference?*

Within faith-based organizations where people believe God's agenda ought to be the bottom line, the answers to these questions are discerned as you listen together for what God is saying to you. Bible study, therefore, will be a big part of the process. Together, you will listen for what God is saying to you through Scripture, as well as the through the things you say to each other in holy conversation and the things you hear your neighbor saying.

An umbrella strategy doesn't lay out a plan or give you a map for your journey. In fact, it assumes that you can't possibly predict where your journey will take you. But having an umbrella strategy will give people in your organization confidence as they take this journey together. It will be easier to go with the flow, following wherever God seems to be leading, if it doesn't feel like you're getting jerked down every minor tributary on the river.

So, let's have a closer look at the three components of an umbrella strategy,

1. A SENSE OF PURPOSE

Purpose is the reason you or your organization exists. French philosophers use the phrase "raison d'être"—your reason for being. In a faith-based organization, a clear sense of purpose not only helps you focus your work in a way that makes a difference to God, it comes from God.

Effective organizations are able to articulate their purpose clearly. Everybody in the organization knows what it is. Leaders watch for opportunities to act, but test their possible actions with questions like: *Is this action consistent with our purpose? Does it help us do what we are here to do?* Only if the answer is yes do they move ahead.

In some ways, your purpose is like the keel on a sailboat. Without it the boat will skate across the surface of the water, at the mercy of the winds, out of control, with no traction for maintaining any sense of direction on the water. But with the keel in place, the boat's hull grips the water and can go where it needs to go.

> *"Your purpose is the reason you or your organization exists."*

Although his followers remember him explaining it in various ways, the New Testament tells us that Jesus is a good example of someone who was very clear about his purpose. He knew why he was here:

"Let us go on to the neighboring towns, so that I may proclaim the message there also; for that is what I came to do." (Mark 1:38)

"I have come to call not the righteous but sinners." (Mark 2:17b)

"I have come as light into the world, so that everyone who believes

in me should not remain in the darkness." (John 12:46)
"For this I was born, and for this I came into the world, to testify
to the truth." (John 18:37b)

"'The Spirit of the Lord is upon me, because he has anointed
me to bring good news to the poor. He has sent me to proclaim
release to the captives and recovery of sight to the blind, to let the
oppressed go free, to proclaim the year of the Lord's favor.' And he
rolled up the scroll, gave it back to the attendant, and sat down.
The eyes of all in the synagogue were fixed on him. Then he began
to say to them, 'Today this scripture has been fulfilled in your
hearing.'" (Luke 4:18-21)

However he said it, it is clear that Jesus' purpose was connected to
God's mission in the world. In fact, in John's version of the story,
Jesus says straight out: "I have come down from heaven, not to do
my own will, but the will of him who sent me." (John 6:38).

Likewise, our purpose is connected to what God is up to in
the world. Jesus came to open our eyes to the inbreaking of a new
world where blind see, deaf hear, lame walk and captives are freed.
These things are happening right here, right now. "For, in fact, the
kingdom of God is among you!" Jesus proclaims (Luke 17:21b),
and we are invited to participate in it.

There is more and more agreement across denominations
that the personal work of Jesus was primarily centered on making
the kingdom of God present and helping people see it. His
own sense of purpose was centered there and all of his teaching,
healing and other work was focused on making it happen. The
incarnation (God coming "in the flesh") is all about how God
in Jesus is doing this. God comes to be involved and at work in
the world that God has made and loves. Jesus starts out early
to find people who will join him in this work. The ministry of

Jesus makes it clear that God is at work in the world and God wants people to be partners and co-creators in that work.

This invitation to partnership, to co-create with God, is the starting point of your own unique purpose in this world. You are invited to join with God in the mission to bless, heal, reconcile and love the world. You are called to work with God in the places where God's work is unfolding in your context. That is where you find your purpose.

Claiming your purpose with heartfelt commitment and naming it clearly can help your faith-based organization begin to see why it exists and what it can do to contribute to what God is already doing.

Are people in your congregation or faith-based organization clear about their purpose? Here are some questions you can ask yourself to find out:

Can most of the people in our organization describe our shared purpose in eight words or less?

Do our leaders intentionally make important decisions on the basis of that shared purpose?

Do our leaders ever say no to something because it does not support and/or conflicts with our shared purpose?

When our leaders are chosen, is it because they are wholeheartedly committed to our shared purpose?

Are most of the people in our organization excited enough about our shared purpose to make sacrifices and/or take holy risks for the sake of it?

Share this list of questions with your other leaders and see what they think. In many faith-based organizations, people assume they have a shared sense of purpose that they don't really have, and it's been a long time since they talked about it together.

2. A SET OF GUIDING PRINCIPLES

Most of us had an experience like this growing up. You had a friend or group of friends who wanted to do something that your parents thought was questionable. You pressed and pressed, trying to get your way so you could do it. Eventually, tired of hearing that "everyone else is allowed to do it," your mom or someone said, "I don't care what everyone else is doing. You're not everyone else and we don't do that in this family!"

When you heard those words you knew that you were crossing the line from being who you are to being someone else, and your folks weren't going to let you go there. That's a little like what a guiding principle does.

A set of guiding principles is an important component in an umbrella strategy. Guiding principles deepen your sense of who you are and help clarify what you are about. They are a little different from core values, which explain what you believe. Guiding principles say what really matters to you and guide your every decision and your every action. One way to think about it is that a core value is a noun and a guiding principle is a verb.

Guiding principles contain the foundational commitments that frame your identity and shape your behavior. Like your core values, they stand at the center of who you are. They demand more of you than mere ideological assent. They are as visible in your actions as they are in the words you use.

When you articulate your guiding principles, you are not painting a picture of who you would like to be sometime in the future. You are making a statement that describes your deepest self, right now in the present. When you do something that somehow makes you look different than the picture you paint with these guiding principles, you know you have gotten distracted and failed to be who you are.

> *"Guiding principles contain the foundational commitments that frame your identity and shape your behavior."*

Often, guiding principles have been discovered more than they have been decided. In some ways, that's how it happened for that earliest church. You can see their guiding principles emerging as they go with the flow, following where the Spirit leads them.

Jesus gave them a pretty clear purpose: *You shall be my witnesses*. They had a sense of direction: *Start in Jerusalem, then go to Judea and Samaria and to the ends of the earth*.

But it wasn't until Peter was standing in the kitchen of a Gentile soldier and his family, watching the Spirit fill them up, that he realized what really mattered to him; It wasn't the rule book that said you can't eat pork, especially with somebody who's unclean; it wasn't making all of his Jewish friends back in Jerusalem happy; it wasn't the tradition of his fathers. For Peter, what really mattered was following the Spirit. He took that back to the council in Jerusalem and what emerged was the articulation of a new guiding principle: *Do what seems right to us and to the Holy Spirit* (Acts 15:28).

Throughout the rest of the story, you can see guiding principles at work in the life of the early church. It is equally important to spend time as you go, discovering and articulating your guiding principles together. They can help you be more accountable to yourself and the purpose for which you have been formed in your organization.

Most organizations find that a few short statements (three to seven bullet points), that accurately share their values and shape their behaviors and decision-making, can help them stay purposefully focused on the work they are meant to do.

Does your organization have a set of guiding principles that articulate your values in ways that guide decisions and shape behaviors? What follows are some indicators that an organization understands its guiding principles and uses them well. How many of these are true in your organization?:

Leaders in our organization have spent time discussing and reflecting on our guiding principles and how they should be lived out. We even have a clear list for our common work together.

People can talk easily and with clarity about the guiding principles that shape our organization. Leaders can tell stories about how our guiding principles were discovered and/or how they have been put to use in times of trouble, at turning points in our life together or when major decisions have been made.

Most of our participants understand the guiding principles well enough that we are able to share them clearly and help people use them to start new groups, teams and projects without needing permission from an offical structure—the clarity has removed the hoops to jump through and provided a "permission-granted" system.

3. A SET OF STRATEGIC DIRECTIONS

A third component in your umbrella strategy is a set of strategic directions. Typically, a strategic direction is very different from a goal that you hope to achieve in the future. It is, rather, a broad statement that points you in a particular direction so that you know where to focus and what to do right now: *Combat hunger,* for example; or *address rural despair*; or *cultivate leadership*. Notice that a set of strategic directions (unlike a strategic plan) doesn't dictate how you'll go about doing it. It doesn't define the objective. It doesn't even presume to know what the objective ought to be exactly—you usually won't discover that until you're moving along, engaging your context, in the flow. In fact, sometimes, you won't know what the goal should have been until you've already reached it and you can look back and say, "Oh, so that's where we've been headed!" A strategic direction is just that—a *direction* in which you have committed to go in order to do what matters right now in God's emerging future.

For faith-based organizations, your sense of direction (just like your purpose and principles) comes from God. You can discern the direction God wants you to move by paying attention to the assets, wows and needs within your organization and in your community. The truth is, there are all kinds of good things you and your organization could be doing. But if you try to do everything, you'll most likely end up doing nothing at all.

Having strategic directions will help you focus your resources in a way that makes a difference right now. At the same time, your strategic directions shouldn't suffocate you or stifle the creativity of people in your organization. If something new emerges and you sense the Spirit leading you, follow! And, by all means, revisit your strategic directions regularly. Ask questions like: *Is this where God seems to be leading us? Does a new direction seem to be emerging? Is this something that really matters? Is this what God wants us to be doing right now?* At least once every few years stand still for awhile as an organization and, in an intentional way, listen together for God's direction.

> *"Strategic directions are broad statements that focus your attention and resources in a way that makes a difference right now."*

Your strategic directions should be especially helpful in giving focus to your leaders. Often it's helpful to have a team, task force and/or staff responsible for stewarding the work in each strategic direction. But these directions should inform the work of every leader, no matter what their role is, across the whole organization. Again, that early church gives us a picture of how this works. Their strategic directions came from Jesus. He said *be my witnesses:*

- *in Jerusalem;*
- *in Judea and Samaria;*
- *to the ends of the earth.*

The way the book of Acts tells the story, James stayed in Jerusalem; Peter went to the Gentiles; Paul went to Rome, and from there planned to head to Spain and the (known) ends of the earth. The fact that you are reading this book and doing the work you do is evidence that, although Paul never made it, others did. In other words, God made sure those early leaders divided up responsibility for each of the strategic directions Jesus articulated for them. At the same time, they each did their work with the others in mind. Peter went back to Jerusalem to discuss the Gentile strategy; Paul took up a collection to create and nurture relationships between Jerusalem and the church 'out there.' Each one was responsible for a particular direction and for the whole.

Working with strategic directions can be confusing for leaders who are used to traditional strategic plans. One agency director grew exasperated as we tried to explain how to use an umbrella strategy in his work. *But what do I measure?* he asked. *How do I know if we're making progress?* It was clear to him that the old way of measuring progress—*Are we beating out the competition? Do we have more butts and bucks than we did last year?*—would be meaningless if he engaged this kind of journey. He's not alone—we encounter this question all the time. In a renewable way of working together you'll measure things that really matter instead. You'll ask questions like:

What are we learning as we pursue our strategic directions?

Is our capacity to make a difference growing?

What is changing as a result of our efforts?

How are we being changed by this journey together?

What has happened to the leadership capacity of our organization as a result of our work?

What new things seem to be emerging within each direction?

Are there other directions that seem to be emerging?

How are we going to respond to that?

In a renewable approach, learning itself is an outcome because the things you learn will inform your journey and better equip you to sense where the Spirit is leading you next.

Does your organization have a sense of direction? Is your life and work being shaped by God's direction for you? Ask yourself:

Have we spent time listening together for where God wants us to focus our attention and resources for the sake of doing what matters right here and right now?

Can we articulate a set of strategic directions?

Do our leaders use these directions to inform our staffing, budget and programing?

Is someone responsible and accountable for stewarding our work in each strategic direction?

Can our people describe the difference we've made in each of our directions?

Are lives being changed as a result of our efforts in each direction?

If you do not have an umbrella strategy in place in your organization, create one.[4] This is the lens that helps you make sense of everything you're seeing as you keep your eyes open for what God is up to in your context.

---

[4] A consulting group like ARE can help you do this.

CHAPTER FOUR
SEEING WITH YOUR NEIGHBOR'S EYES

"The PAWN process teaches you to discover what God's agenda is..."

Feeding the homeless and making sure they get decent health care is challenging enough. But what about actually changing the policies that keep people impoverished? What about mobilizing the poorest of the poor to challenge the state, improve their own living conditions and promote their own rights? That is the radical idea behind The Society for the Promotion of Area Resource Centers (SPARC)[5] and its partners, who are now operating in nine states in one of the poorest countries in the world—India. Since 1984, this organization has been mobilizing and resourcing poor people, especially mothers (who are often willing to act fearlessly for the sake of their children), to gain access to housing and the rights of citizenship. Today they serve over 750,000 households across the country, and their efforts have been so successful they have attracted the attention of slum dweller organizations around the globe. Together with SPARC, these organizations have formed a larger network called Shack/Slum Dwellers International (SDI).

One of the keys to SPARC's success is that its priorities as an organization are established by the communities of poor people they serve; poor people are partners and participants in this work, not recipients of a handout. In fact, the only non-negotiable SPARC had when it began was its commitment to working with the poorest of the urban poor. It was up to the communities themselves to decide what SPARC was going to focus on and how they were going to get it done together.[6]

[5] Visit the SPARC website at http://www.sparcindia.org
[6] Nivedita Sharma, "Securing shelter: hope for Mumbai's slums, City Life." http://www.wfsnews.org/citylife/inside.html

Unfortunately, the conditions that allowed SPARC to thrive and grow in its early years are changing. According to Sheela Patel (the founding director of SPARC), the organizations that fund the kind of work she's doing "have become more focused on developing portfolios of projects, managing risks and producing outcomes rather than on listening to communities, healing deep inequities and supporting innovation."[7]

The nonprofit agencies and foundations that provide grant monies to organizations like SPARC have become more and more professionalized; their leaders think their education, conceptual expertise and position make them most qualified to determine the goals, strategies and plans of the organizations they are funding. People like Patel feel like they are increasingly being viewed as contractors, hired to deliver the visions of their funders, rather than as innovators and change makers. Just imagine how the poor people whose leadership has made SPARC so effective for the past two and a half decades are viewed.

AN UNBUTTONED-DOWN APPROACH

One of the biggest mistakes leaders can make is to be too certain of their own importance, too confident in their own abilities, and too sure that they have all the answers. This happens in faith-based organizations as often as it happens anywhere else. That's why when we begin a project with an organization, one of the first things we ask the board or steering team members to do is loosen their ties—literally—or metaphorically if they don't

---

[7] Sheela Patel tells her own story and describes the shift in the way NGOs and foundations are working in the article, "The Wrong Risks," *Stanford Social Innovation Review*, December 15, 2009. http://www.ssireview.org/articles/entry/the_wrong_risks

actually have one on. Using the PAWN process to pay attention to what God is doing requires a decidedly *un*buttoned-down approach.

The PAWN process assumes that your agenda is not and should not be the most important thing. God's agenda is. Just as startlingly, the PAWN process teaches you how to discover what God's agenda is by paying attention to what God is up to 'out there' in your context, in and through the lives of your neighbors.

BRINGING IT ALL TOGETHER

There isn't anything unique, of course, about asking an organization to take its context into consideration as it figures out how to move forward. It is, in fact, standard operating procedure for organizations that have been shaped by a modern, industrial mindset. This includes most faith-based organizations and churches where the primary concern is having more of an impact, attracting a bigger share of the market, becoming more relevant to a changing neighborhood and/or connecting with people in an emerging culture for the sake of institutional growth.

Throughout the 1990s, for example, according to official Presbyterian Church USA denominational reports, these kinds of explicit ministry goals were "part and parcel of the Presbyterian experience." The top objective, set by 74% of goal-setting Presbyterian congregations in 1998, was to "attract and enlist new members."[8]

---

[8] James Guinn, Presbyterian Mission Statements and Explicit Ministry Goals, 1999. http://www.pcusa.org/research/monday/missstat.htm

In order to meet these kinds of goals, modern church leaders have been convinced of the importance of "reading the audience" (e.g., doing environmental scans, collecting copious demographic data, identifying "opportunities" and "threats" using a SWOT Analysis.).

Problem Alert

This is the title of a class that has been a graduation requirement for every MDiv student at one of the largest mainline seminaries in North America for nearly a decade. In fact, one of our team members actually taught that class for several years.

Problem Alert

A SWOT Analysis is a popular 20th century tool used in corporate planning. It gathers data on the "strengths" and "weaknesses" inside the company; and the "opportunities" and "threats" in your environment. This data is used to establish goals and objectives, in decision making, in crisis prevention and management, etc. It is used in many non-profit and faith-based organizations, as well.

The PAWN process is not unique in asking you to pay attention to your context. What differentiates it is the ways in which it asks you to understand and relate to your context. It refuses to let you see your environment as a threat to be dealt with, even when it feels like resources are scarce. It will not let you view other organizations in your context as competitors. It prevents you from seeing your neighbors as a 'target audience' that you need to attract, reach, enlist, help or convert. Instead, the PAWN process urges you to see your neighbors as people with whom you are called to have a relationship and through whom God is already working. This way of seeing treats your neighbors as co-creators (or potential co-creators) with you, participating in God's mission to bring reconciliation and freedom to the whole creation. They may or may not be used to seeing what they do as being useful or important to God. The second lens of the PAWN process helps you remember that it is. The neighbor lens ensures that you are paying attention to three important aspects of your neighbors' lives: assets, wows and needs. If you look at the third lens, which focuses on what God is doing in and through you and/ or your organization, you'll notice

Lens #2:
Your Neighbor/Context
A) **A**ssets, gifts and passions
B) **W**ow! Good things already happening
C) **N**eeds of your neighbors

the three components listed in that lens are exactly the same as the ones in the neighbor lens. In other words, this process helps you see *all* human beings as equally valuable to God and universally called to participate in what God is up to.

The first component of the neighbor lens includes all the

Lens #3: You
A) **A**ssets, gifts and passions
B) **W**ow! Good things already happening
C) **N**eeds in your life/organization

things God has given to your neighbors to work with, their "assets, gifts and passions." It is represented by the "A" in the PAWN acronym. It is one of the things that grassroots leaders like Sheela Patel, who work with poor and marginalized people, are begging us to pay attention to and take seriously. She wants the groups working with poor people to actually partner with them, not just serve them. She wants us to see how much poor people have to bring to the shared work of making the world a better place.

But even church leaders who work in contexts filled with rich and privileged people often fail to see their neighbors this way. Instead, leaders in faith-based groups tend to focus on sharing what they have—from good news to good deeds—with their neighbors. This is a seemingly noble cause that effectively objectifies their neighbors. Without meaning to, it misses all that these neighbors have to offer.

We've found that it is a very rare thing, indeed, for a faith-based organization to have a sense that their purpose includes joining with their neighbors in what God is already doing in and through their context; their efforts are almost exclusively one-directional. The second arrow in the PAWN process, and the reminder to pay attention to the assets, gifts and passion of your neighbors, helps correct that.

The idea that their neighbor might be able to use what they have to offer and be a co-creator with them in God's mission is foreign to many faith-based leaders. In some cases we've even had church leaders reject this idea as absurd, even somehow heretical. But the biblical story is filled with examples of how God was at work in and through people who were outside of the faith community. Just look at the history of Israel: One of the first things King Cyrus of Persia did after defeating the Babylonians was to set free

Problem Alert

One Roman Catholic church in Florida, for example, says, "Our mission is to carry the gospel, the sacraments, and God's love and fellowship to the unchurched, the alienated and the excommunicated (the church's homeless)." A CME church in Alaska says they are "Reaching out to the World...Preaching to the Unsaved... Teaching the Saved to Serve." A United Methodist church in Alabama says their purpose is "To grow in faith and share our faith in God with the world around us." A UCC congregation in Oregon says, "In addition to worshipping, educating ourselves and opening our doors to everyone (no exceptions): We are called to share the Good News of the Gospel and minister to our community and to the world." [9]

[9] See more at www.missionstatements.com

the Israelites, who had been living in exile and serving as slaves to the Babylonian empire (Ezra). King Artaxerxes sent his servant Nehemiah to Jerusalem—with supplies!—to oversee the rebuilding of the city walls and the Temple, which had been destroyed by their enemies (Nehemiah). The Jewish festival of Purim remembers the salvation that came to them through the actions of King Ahasuerus (Esther).

It's enough to make you say, "Wow!"— which is also the second component in the neighbor lens, represented by the "W" in the PAWN acronym. Wows are the amazing things God is already doing in and through your neighbors. When your eyes are open to what God is up to 'out there,' you see parents in your local elementary school who deeply love and care for their children. You find talented people whose work makes a huge contribution to the quality of life (including your own) in your community. And you find people who give their time and talent and donate money to causes that touch your heart, too. Many of your neighbors would describe what they do and why they do it and never think to mention God. But you know better. God is at work in these people, helping them do amazing things. Your job is to keep your eyes open for it so that you can name it when you see it and join in, in whatever ways you can.

Not everything that is happening in your context is making God smile, of course. There are many, many things that are breaking God's heart. The third component of the neighbor lens helps keep your eyes open to those things by focusing your attention on your neighbors' "Needs," represented by the "N" in the PAWN acronym. It's important to remember that your neighbors have needs, regardless of the setting you are working in. Faith-based organizations have often done best in identifying the needs of poor people who struggle for jobs, food and shelter. These needs are often obvious—even to the casual observer. But there are needs in every setting; they can just be harder to see in more affluent contexts where it looks like everything is going right.

Paying attention to what is breaking God's heart in your context can help point to where and how you can be most useful to God right now.

Problem Alert

The public unveiling of Tiger Woods' apparently perfect private life revealed a shocking emptiness and tremendous amount of pain.

The second arrow in the PAWN process prevents you from making the mistake of thinking you've got all the answers (or that you even need to have them all) by reminding you to pay attention to what God is up to in and through your neighbors. It helps shape the way you see everything, what you decide to do and how you do it. Once you learn to see things this way, it will seem unnatural to just do things *for* your neighbors; you'll want to do what matters to God *with* them.

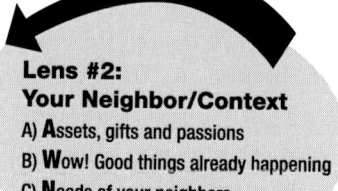

**Lens #2:
Your Neighbor/Context**
A) **A**ssets, gifts and passions
B) **W**ow! Good things already happening
C) **N**eeds of your neighbors

You won't even think about starting up a new program or ministry unless you've also explored the possibility of jumping in on a meaningful project that is already happening in your community. You'll smile at the things God is smiling at. And when God's heart breaks, yours will too. That pain will compel you to work with your neighbors to make a difference in their lives and in the life of the world.

Of course, none of this is possible unless you actually get to know your neighbors.

GETTING PRACTICAL

Paying attention to what God is up to in the world around you is not something you do once, as part of a strategic planning process for example. It is about getting to know your neighbors and building relationships with them in an ongoing way. It is about keeping your eyes and ears open to what is and what seems to be emerging everywhere you go in your community. But there are some simple first steps you can take to begin getting to know what's happening in your context. Not all of these suggestions will make sense for your organization or necessarily work in your context, but some of them probably will. This isn't meant to be an exhaustive list. Nor is it a checklist that you have to follow in lock-step fashion. These suggestions are meant to help you begin to imagine ways that you can get to know your neighbors for the sake of discovering what God is up to and how you can be useful to God in your context:

Map It!

If your organization is working in a particular geographic location, get a map of the area you see as the focus for your work. You may need to do some thinking about what that area is. Are there natural boundaries that give shape to your area—a river, railroad tracks, divided highways? Are there demographic connections around ethnicity or economics that are relevant? Where do school district lines fall and do they impact relationships? What issues are there that impact people connecting, working together and experiencing each other as neighbors on the same journey? If you are looking at a large area like a state or province, what are some of the key sub-units that you may need to pay attention to (multiple urban areas, urban/rural contexts)?

Make it Real

Drive or walk (or both) around the area you are working in; for now, just look and observe. What are the key landmarks? What kinds of services (e.g., fire stations, police stations, parks, schools, grocery stores) are available in the community? On your map, locate and label all of these things. Ask yourself what's missing. Who else is working to make a difference in your community (e.g., agencies, clubs, resident associations, civic groups, religious groups, government agencies)? What relational connections do people in your community have with people beyond the map? For example, if there is an elementary school within your neighborhood but no high school, some people in your community are connected to that out of area school as well (including relationships, services and facilities there). This map is not meant to limit you; it should have blurry edges. People on the map are naturally connected to people off the map; try to get a sense of what those relationships look like. You should expect this map to change over time as you develop new relationships and discover new things about your context. Keep it handy.

Do the Numbers

Demographic data won't do much to help you get to know your neighbors, but it can help you know what kinds of questions to ask. Spend a little time gathering it. Many denominations have access to detailed zip code or postal code reports and provide them to congregations at no cost. These reports are also available online. If in the USA, use any online search engine, type in "zip code data," and you'll get links to multiple sources for this information. In Canada, you can obtain the most accurate information on the Statistics Canada website, www.statcan.gc.ca. If you're part of an organization that spans a very large area (e.g., state, province or region) you may benefit from using a provider to get more nuanced data and/or some guidance in analyzing it.

Depending on some things you decided when you made your map, you may want to visit city and county planning departments, your chamber of commerce or appropriate state/provincial planning agencies to get a picture of what seems to be emerging in your community in terms of planning, business promotion, housing development, etc.

Once you have gathered the data, look for patterns. What are you seeing in terms of race and ethnicity, educational levels, age distribution, housing, employment and socio-economic levels? How does what's happening in your community compare with the rest of the region you're a part of? Is your community more or less diverse than the region? More or less educated? Older or younger? Richer or poorer? As you're looking at the data, write down your reflections and the questions it raises for you. Do this on your own and with a group of leaders from your organization. Use these questions as a starting point:

What do I want to know more about?

Who do I need to talk to in order to find out more?

What is unsettling to me about what I've found so far?

What is exciting to me about this data?

What don't I understand?

What is God saying to me through what I've discovered?

Get Out of Here

One of the reasons a lot of leaders haven't met their neighbors is because they never get out of the building. Jesus spent most of his time out in public spaces where he could meet people. Try it. Here are five ways you can get out there. Let them inspire you to think of even more:

1. Go visiting

Take out your map and pick an area to go visiting. We're serious. Just walk up to a front door and knock. See if someone answers. If they do, introduce yourself. "Hi, my name is _____ and I'm part of _____ church/organization. We're your neighbors and thought we ought to get to know you." People will expect the pitch. You know, the one about being saved or going to heaven or whatever. Surprise them by not giving it to them. In fact, unless they bring it up, don't even talk about your faith, how great your organization is, or anything else 'religious.' Do not—we repeat—Do not sell Jesus to them! Just get to know them.

If you live in a city, you may want to pick a street corner, bus stop or other gathering place to have these conversations. Say something like, "I'm trying to meet our neighbors and get to know you. Have you got a minute to help me learn some more about this community?" Then, if they say "yes," (and many will!) ask them the kinds of questions the PAWN process raises (e.g., assets, wows and needs). Really listen to them. Ask good follow-up questions. Remember that God has something to say to you through them. Pay attention. Here are some good questions to ask your neighbors:

What do you like about living here? What are the best things about this community?

Who are the unsung heros in this community—the people who are making a positive difference?

What would make this community a better place to live?

Thank them before you leave and ask them if they'd like to be added to your mailing list; that way they can see what you're up to and what happens as a result of what you're learning.

The next time you go visiting, take somebody from your organization along with you. It'll help open their eyes to what God is up to and it'll be more fun. Do this regularly.

2. Talk to more people

A second way to get to know what God is up to in your community is to talk one-on-one with people who have specific insights. Make a list of who those people are. Use the demographic data you gathered, the things you observed while you were driving around and the things you heard from your neighborhood visits to figure out who you need to be talking to. Your list might include: the mayor of your town or your city council representative, the principal of the school down the street or the school board president, the fire captain or police officer who covers your streets, the city or county planner, social service executives, service providers who work with poor or marginalized people, interfaith religious leaders.

In most cases, if you call these people on the phone or walk into their office to set up an appointment, they will be glad to talk to you. Simply explain who you are and that you are trying to get a better understanding of the community so that you can be a better neighbor and help make a difference. Most will be honored that you noticed they have expertise in the community.

The discussions with these people will not be too different

from the ones you have with neighborhood residents. You should ask about assets, gifts and passions; the good stuff (i.e., wows!) already happening and the needs people in the community are facing. Take good notes. Here are some examples of questions you might ask:

What do you see as the biggest strengths of our community?

What individuals and/or organizations do you think are really making a positive difference here?

What are the biggest issues facing our community and the people who live here?

What things do you think a helpful church/organization could do to benefit this community?

What could we do to make your work more effective?

Be prepared to act on what you hear. Go meet the people who you learn are making a difference; go find out what their organizations are doing; follow up in ways that you are told will make a difference; share what you're learning with others in your community and within your organization; pay attention to what seems to be emerging and get ready to join in.

3. Network

A third way to get to know what God is up to in your context is to network with other leaders who are making a difference. They may be a part of a civic group (e.g., Lions, Kiwanis, Rotary) or a community group (e.g., local residents' organization, a historical society, scouting groups, etc.). Some of these organizations may provide services within the same arena as you do; they will be your peers. Some will be working in other arenas but will offer insight that you wouldn't otherwise have. A few may be organizations that you already have a connection to (e.g., the council at the school where you tutor, the scouting group that meets in your space, the housing project you've partnered with in the past).

Ask the leader of the group if they would let you have a few minutes during a meeting. Explain that you see them as valuable partners in the work you are doing, that you appreciate the work they do and the insights they bring, that you want to know what they know and would be honored if they'd take the time to share it. If they say yes, use the same kinds of questions you asked residents and community leaders. Listen to what they have to say. Reflect on what you're hearing God say to you through their stories, insights and questions.

4. Hang out

Think about what you observed as you wandered around your community. Where do people gather? Where does gossip get started or passed on? Where are friendships made? Where is wisdom collected? Where are perspectives shaped? In a small town it may be a locally-owned diner or a donut shop. In a city, it may be a chain coffee shop with a wireless internet hotspot that attracts people who sit, talk and work there. It may be a barber shop, a group of benches in a local park, the walking path in your local mall, the Friday night high school football game, the library, a gym, the dog park, your local pub or a knitting group.

Go where you're comfortable and do what feels natural. Have fun! Explore your own passions and meet people who share them. In these settings, you're probably not going to ask formal questions (although the opportunity to host an informal focus group might suddenly present itself—be ready!). Be open to talking with people. Listen to them and what you're hearing God say to you through them. In the flow of what's happening ask questions. Build relationships and get to know them and their friends. In a word—learn.

5. Listen to your own people

Over our sometimes rocky history, some sort of wall has been built between the church and the world. This wall is often physical and real—the bricks and mortar of a church building where people gather to be religious 'in there,' while non-religious people continue doing what they do 'out there.' Many a church organization has died hiding behind concrete and stained glass wishing someone from outside would venture in.

But an even bigger wall exists in the minds of many religious people. What they do 'in here' is kept separate from what they do 'out there.' One experience doesn't inform or seem to impact the other.

But once the blinders are removed they'll discover and remember that they are all experts about what is happening in your community (they live there, too!) and their insights can help you pay attention to what God is up to. Ask the people who are part of your faith community what they know, who they know and what they see. Use the same kinds of questions you used when you went visiting. Listen.

The second lens of the PAWN process reminds you to keep your eyes and ears open to what God is up to in and through your neighbors. Wherever you go and whatever you're doing, expect to see God on the loose and at work. And keep your tie loose (or your clerical collar). Heck, take it off altogether. Do whatever you have to in order to remember that God's agenda is the only one that really matters—and that you need your neighbors in order to discover what God's mission (for you, your organization, your community and the world) seems to be.

CHAPTER FIVE
SEEING YOURSELF WITH NEW EYES

"We're sick of seeing congregations trying to be something they're not, striving for goals they will never reach and killing themselves to offer the services and programs they think they have to provide in order to be competitive."

There is a little Presbyterian church in central Florida that, on an average Sunday, used to look like thousands of other mainline congregations in North America. About thirty-five people, most over the age of seventy-five, gathered for worship in a beautiful and much beloved building that, sadly, now felt way too big and empty. They had tried everything to grow their church but they were exhausted. Then a local youth organization asked if they could use the building for an after-school program. You could just hear the Alleluia choir singing! *There'll be children here again!* Until, that is, people found out that the youth this organization serves are at-risk gay and lesbian teenagers.

(Cue sound effect: *screeching halt.*)

What happened next probably never would have happened if one of the women in the church hadn't stood up and told everybody, for the first time, that her middle-aged daughter was a lesbian and that it always hurt that she'd felt unwelcome in the church. She wished, when her daughter had been a teenager, there had been a safe and loving place for her somewhere.

Suddenly, everybody started talking about a family member or a friend who had experienced the same discrimination because of sexual orientation or something else. Before you knew it the people in that little congregation had decided to put their prized possession to good use; they opened the doors of their building to those teens. They got to know the people who ran the club. They made friends. And they invited their new friends to worship. Some of them came and they brought their friends with them. They're still bringing them.

One of the members of this congregation, a ninety-four-year-old great-great-grandmother, told us that one Sunday recently there were so many people at worship that when they held hands for the final blessing they made a circle that stretched clear around the whole sanctuary. There wasn't a missing link anywhere. She looked around the room at all the new faces—many of whom appeared as strange to her as that Ethiopian eunuch must have seemed to Philip—and she felt tears of joy streaming down her cheeks. Her pastor said something like, "You know, this little church might not be able to do a lot of things it used to be able to do, but these people are grandmothers and grandfathers and great aunts and uncles. And if there is one thing they know how to do, it's how to love."

GETTING REAL

Go to any mainline denominational assembly or conference these days and you'll see the same thing: a lot of gray hair. This reality creates high levels of anxiety for denominational officials and congregational leaders alike. "Hurry!" many of them are saying with more than an edge of panic in their voices, "We have to do something before it's too late!" They race to one church growth program after another trying to find something to save the sinking ship. At the same time, the age and decline of mainline churches has left some leaders depressed and paralyzed by fear.

Personally, we are tired of watching little old ladies (and men)

Problem Alert

One man we know recently told the leaders in his congregation, "Just make sure if you're the last one here you turn the lights off before you leave."

beat themselves up because their congregation can't keep up with the big box church down the street. We are sick of seeing congregations trying to be something they're not, striving for goals they will never reach and killing themselves to offer the services and programs they think they have to provide in order to compete. For that matter, we're pretty fed up with watching big 'successful' churches work people to death, too; leaving one volunteer after another feeling used up and burnt out in the impassioned drive to win the prize of biggest and best.

Jesus calls each of us (and the organizations we care about) to do no more and no less than this:

Be who you are and see what you have for the sake of doing what matters to God.[12]

In other words, if you're a little old lady, then be that in a way that makes a difference to God. If you're a teenager, then be that in a way that is useful to God's mission to love and bless the world. The same goes for your organization. We're not saying you shouldn't dream—even really big dreams. Dare to reach for the stars. But you've relinquished the idea that you can control the outcome of your efforts, remember? Your main priority is doing what matters to God right here and right now; putting who you are and what you have into the service of what God is up to.

The PAWN process is designed to help you do that. It trains you to see who you are and what you have more clearly for the sake of doing what really matters. The first lens helps you make sense of what you're seeing and the second helps you see with your neighbor's eyes. The third lens puts the focus most sharply on you. It invites you to pay attention to what God is up to in your life right now. It prevents you from pining away over who you used to be or daydreaming about what you could do if you only had what someone else has. It focuses your attention on who you really are and what you really have today.

[12] Learning how to do that is the focus of our book _The Future Starts Now: The Renewable Organization for Faith-Based Groups_ (A Renewal Enterprise, 2009).

The first thing you might notice as you study the third lens is that you look remarkably like your neighbors. This shouldn't come as a shock because we've already agreed that God is as much at work 'out

Lens #3: You
A) **A**ssets, gifts and passions
B) **W**ow! Good things already happening
C) **N**eeds in your life/organization

there' among our neighbors as 'in here' with us; that's the testimony of the biblical story, and it's our own experience. Like our neighbors, we have assets (A), wows (W), and needs (N).

THE GREAT EXCUSE

It can be difficult to see the assets, gifts and passions of our neighbors for a variety of reasons. For starters, we often don't know them very well. They also have traditionally been viewed as recipients of ministry and help rather than co-creators with us of a better world. But it can be just as hard to see our own assets, gifts and passions (the first component in the third lens.)

A lot of faith-based groups today are used to operating with a scarcity mindset. They see only what they used to have and don't any longer, what somebody else has that they wish they had, or what they don't have but think they need in order to do what matters. If you've ever sat in on a board meeting at budget time when the most over-used phrase is "we can't," then you know what we're talking about.

Not only is a scarcity mindset an affront to the God who provides and demeaning to the billions of people on this planet who experience real need because of the way our culture hoards and over-consumes resources, this way of thinking makes it impossible to see straight. It clouds your vision and depresses your outlook.

Suddenly a group of talented people with nothing but possibilities ahead becomes blind to opportunities and trapped by "if only" thinking. (e.g., "If only we had more fill-in-the-blank, then we could do what matters.")

It might sound terrible to say, but we suspect that sometimes this way of thinking and operating is nothing more than a smokescreen; it allows people to believe their own illusion that *if* they had the resources *then* they would gladly and energetically implement a great idea. But since they don't have what they need, they can just do nothing, without guilt and without any burden of responsibility. This is what we call The Great Excuse.

Whether or not a scarcity mindset is cynical, it is always tragic. The reality is that God has blessed you and the people in your organization with countless assets, gifts and passions. Why? The author of the letter to the Ephesians put it this way: *...to promote the body's growth in building itself up in love* (Eph. 4:16). In other words, all of those assets, gifts and passions are meant to be put to use in a way that makes a difference to your community and to the world.

Of course, nobody was better at recognizing, naming and calling out the gifts within people than Jesus. *You are the light of the world!* he told a crowd filled with peasants, soldiers and priests. *Don't hide it! Use it to light up the whole house!* (Mat. 5:13-15).

Part of your job as a leader is to recognize, name and call out the assets, gifts and passions God has blessed the people in your organization with. The first component (A) in the third lens of the PAWN process helps you remember to be intentional about that.

The second component (W) helps you pay attention to the good things that God is already doing in and through the people of your organization. You'd think this would come naturally, right? But there is increasing data from across denominations that points to a spiritual void in Christian communities, stemming from an inability to see God at work in the midst of everyday life (and maybe even to believe that God is at work at all!).[13] Unable to see God at work, the drive to be a part of what God is up to is lost as well. How do you participate in something that you aren't sure is happening?

Using this third lens in the PAWN process includes being intentional about reawakening people of faith to God's activity in and through them. It's about helping them see things happening to them and through them that make them say "OK, that has to be the Holy Spirit at work because there is no other way to explain it."

We imagine that's what Ananias said to himself as he was on his way to visit Saul, the guy famous for killing Christians. Ananias had a dream that he was supposed to go lay hands on Saul, curing him of his miracle-induced blindness, so that he could become the Lord's "instrument" (Acts 9:1-19). Do you think Ananias was muttering to himself along the way, *Instrument? I'll give you instrument. How about a blunt instrument right upside his head?* Do you think Ananias thought he was losing his mind? Do you think he was terrified? Probably yes, yes and yes. But he went, anyway. And the rest of the story is history—*our* history, as a matter of fact. What else is there to say when you experience God at work in you and through you except *Wow!*?

Few things create as much excitement in people and the organizations they care about than a renewed sense that God is alive and working in and through them. We have seen light

---

[13] In the Evangelical churches, see research of participants in Natural Church Development or the Willow Creek "REVEAL" study. In the Mainline, see work being done by Diana Butler Bass *(Christianity for the Rest of Us,* 2006) or Kelly Fryer *(Reclaiming the "E" Word: Waking Up To Our Evangelical Identity,* 2008). In the Roman Catholic tradition, see work being done by scholars like Richard Rohr.

bulbs turn on and tears of joy flow as we've worked with people in faith-based organizations to help them recognize and name the Wows within them.

As a leader, you will discover the same thing is probably true among the people you work with. Help them recognize where God is at work and then ask them to share their stories with each other. The same light bulbs and tears of joy that we have seen over and over again are waiting to be released in your setting as well.

It's also important to help people name their needs, the third component (N) of this third lens. Often no one wants to acknowledge their needs because needs are viewed purely as negatives and, in faith-based organizations, are sometimes seen as undesirable side effects of sin.

But, believe it or not, needs aren't all bad! Some needs are those things in your life together that are breaking God's heart and your own. These needs cause life to be diminished in significant ways, and pain and suffering may even be the result. But other needs just mean we need help. They provide a connection to others that would not otherwise exist and, in so doing, form the basis for most friendships and communities. Needs are part of what bring people together. We find meaning in meeting the needs of others. We feel loved when our needs are met. Being needy isn't the same as being sinful. To be alive is to be needy. Neediness is part of the fabric of life. This is how it's been from the very beginning.

The way the Hebrew scriptures tell the story, for example, God created a human being (Adam) to help meet God's need for a co-creator. Together, they planted and tilled a garden (Genesis 2:4-8). From the beginning God's world included needs. *It's not good for you to be alone,* God said

(Genesis 2:18). So God created animals and birds to make sure the human would not be alone and then God created another human to be a partner in the work of creation (Genesis 2:19-20).

Jesus says that the heart of life is grounded in the Great Commandment: *You shall love the Lord Your God with all your heart and soul and mind, and you shall love your neighbor as yourself* (Matthew 22:34-40). Life is about relationships, grounded in love, where you do not hold back from one another but, rather, freely give and freely receive. Your needs open you up to these relationships. The needs of others make it possible for you to give yourself away for the sake of making a difference. And your needs make it possible—even necessary—for you to open yourself up to receive what your neighbor has to offer.

Paying attention to all three components—(A) assets, gifts and passions, (W) wows, and (N) needs—in your organization is part of discovering what God is up to so that you can do what matters right here and right now. It prevents you from longing for yesterday or wishing for tomorrow. It helps keep you real.

GETTING PRACTICAL

During those standing still times, when you're discerning an umbrella strategy for your organization (see page 52), you'll want to gather data about the Assets, Wows and Needs of your organization using focus groups, one-on-one interviews and surveys. You'll ask similar questions to the ones you'll ask your neighbors:

What do you see as the biggest strengths of our organization? What individuals and/or groups do you think are really making a positive difference here?

What are the things people care most about and how can these be tapped to make a difference?

What are the most amazing things you've seen happen here as a result of our work together?

What are the biggest issues facing our organization and the people who belong to it?

What are the biggest needs facing us in our life together?

But paying attention to what God is doing in and through you and your organization isn't something you do once; it's an ongoing process. The following are some exercises that you can use to help train yourselves to see your own assets, wows and needs. Not every activity will make sense in every setting and, like the suggestions in the previous chapter, these are meant mostly to spark your imagination. Think about all of the opportunities you have to help people recognize and name their Assets, Wows and Needs. Use them. Get creative. Have fun.

Map this, too!

This exercise doesn't involve an actual street map. This is about discovering and 'mapping' the assets and gifts in a group of people to help them think about what they have to work with. Sometimes, people in faith-based organizations have a hard time naming what they have to offer because they have this strange (and unbiblical!) idea that only certain gifts really count. Sure, the Bible says that God gives the gift of preaching and teaching. But King David was a musician and Dorcas loved to sew (Acts 9:39).

Mapping is a simple technique in which each item inventoried is given its own label. This can be done using mapping software and manipulated with a computer. Or they can be put on individual sticky notes and stuck on a wall. We like the notes and wall method the best. It is a great, playful way to get people thinking and interacting with each other. You can do this exercise during a standing still time but it's fun and helpful to do it anytime a group is trying to get something done.

Here's how asset mapping works: Someone facilitates the group thinking about what it has. This is done by asking a variety of questions about assets and gifts; physical skills, interests, talents, relationships—a wide variety of things that people have at their disposal. People write their answers on sticky notes—one answer per note. After everyone has listed their assets and gifts, they are invited to post them on a wall. This gets everything up and in plain view. For a lot

> Two great resources for more on this topic are *The Power of Asset Mapping: How Your Congregation Can Act on Its Gifts* by Luther Snow (Alban Institute, 2004) and *Asset Building and Community Development* by Gary Paul Green and Anna Haines (Sage Publications, 2007).

of groups, this is a great place to just stop and let what is on the wall sink in. For a group that has a mindset of scarcity and thinks it doesn't have much to work with, just letting a dozen people in a room put up ten notes each means that suddenly what was "not much to work with" is a hundred and twenty things at your disposal. Many a depressed group of people have found their spirits bolstered by just getting this far in the process (usually less than thirty minutes in).

Once everyone has let it soak in that there are all sorts of things to work with, let them start brainstorming all the possible actions that could result if they actually did something with the things they have. Get them to move the notes around the wall and group them together in different ways. You can find groups of notes that are similar (say "reading") and start a book group. But the best ideas are collections of unlike items that create projects which involve people and gifts that are not so similar. For example, a play requires people who like to build sets, write scripts, act, read, promote and sell, run lights and sound, etc.

Only by looking at the diverse things that you have can you put together some of the most interesting and amazing stuff. Group assets, discover possibilities, document what they are and what you used, then put all the sticky notes back on the wall and do it again, looking for more possibilities. Most groups will come up with a ton of ideas. But the most amazing thing is that every idea here is possible.

The following are some questions you could ask to get an asset mapping session started. Remember, have people use one sticky note per answer.

List three things you like to do for fun.

List three things you are good at.

List two things you used to like to do but got too busy and stopped doing.

List two things you would let us use to do something with.

List one person from outside our organization who owes you a favor.

Add your own questions to the list.

Fan the flames

We've discovered that just asking people about assets and gifts isn't enough to find out what God is up to in people or in an organization. To put a gift to use where there is no passion is like putting a square peg in a round hole. You may get it in but it will be painful and you might break something! Passions are the path for square pegs to find square holes. If you discover a person's passion and can help her pursue it, she will use every asset and gift she has to make it happen. In other words, passion is the key to releasing a person's gifts and assets.

The best way to find out what people are passionate about is to ask them. Unlike asset mapping, where everybody has a lot to contribute and you can fill up a whole wall with sticky notes, a person's passions tend to make up a shorter list. This is a list of the things that make a person's heart race. It's the kind of thing most people need a one-on-one conversation or a small group setting to share.

One faith community we've worked with has shared their passions over dinner. People gathered in one place for appetizers at the beginning of the evening. They mingled a bit. Then they were asked to spend about ten minutes sitting and thinking about the things that are most important to them and write brief notes about these things. Then they were organized into groups of about eight people and sent out on a progressive dinner; each course was served in a different home where people ate and talked about all kinds of things. But they were also encouraged to spend the evening sharing the things they wrote down at the beginning. People who had known each other for a long time discovered important things about the friends they thought they knew. At the end of the night people turned in the notes they had made, giving leaders information about what was most important to them and who cared most about what. But more importantly, people were able to connect with others who had similar passions. Surprising possibilities emerged. Some people went away with a strong sense that they were being called into action. These passions provided important insights as the organization began to define the elements of its umbrella strategy.

Here are some questions you can ask face-to-face or in a small group setting to help discover the passions of the people in your organization:

> *If you could change one thing, and only one thing, about the world in your lifetime, what would it be?*

> *What breaks your heart in our city/village/town and what do you think we should do about it?*

> *What is important enough to you that you'd be willing to work on it?*

Read the fine print

In our work with faith-based organizations across the US and Canada, we find this simple question can produce a 'deer in the headlights' look on people's faces: *Where have you seen God at work in the last week?*

Most Christians are used to listening to someone else tell them where God is and what God is doing. Even pastors sometimes find themselves scouring the internet or raiding their bookshelves, desperately trying to find somebody with something interesting to say about the text they're preaching on next weekend. It just isn't the experience of most Christians, especially in the mainline traditions, to be listening for God's voice or on the lookout for what God is doing in their everyday lives. And it certainly isn't common to talk about it.

An easy place to start with a small group (or even with a big group) to help them see the Wows that are all around them is in your local newspaper. This activity won't help them see what God is doing in their own lives exactly, but it will help them discover that God is doing something, and that's a good place to start. Give a section of the newspaper to each person in the room and ask them to read the articles. As they read, tell them to consider this simple question: *Is this something that makes God smile or breaks God's heart?* If God is smiling, ask them to mark it with a happy face. If God cries, have them mark a sad face. Then give people a chance to share what they found with each other.

This simple activity can turn reading the news into a theological exercise for people. It is useful across generations and is a great way to get youth and their grandparents all sharing what they see God caring most about. But it is also a good reminder that God actually does have an opinion about what goes on. It teaches us to keep our eyes open for what God is doing and what God would like to see done. It can even begin to spur ideas about the kinds of things that your organization could and should be involved in.

Bring it home (Part 1)

The best way to help people keep their eyes open for the Wows in your life together is to open their eyes to what God is doing in and through their own everyday lives. Every chance you get, ask people to answer these two questions:

> *How did God's mission of love, blessing, forgiveness, freedom, healing or peace come to you lately?*

> *How did God's mission come through you lately, making a difference in somebody else's life?*

You can use these questions as an opening devotion at the start of your board or council meetings, during worship, as an icebreaker at the beginning of an educational program or brainstorming session or whenever. We like to have people draw their answers to these questions and then share their drawings with each other. It makes the whole experience more playful and, because people are actually looking at how God showed up in and through their lives, more meaningful. Get people seeing the Wows every day and they'll learn to see what God is up to in and through the things your organization does together.

Bring it home (Part 2)

Asking people to pay attention to the needs your organization has, believing that God might in fact be speaking to them through those needs, is a tall order if people equate needs with sin (or something else bad). Start on the personal level, helping people see their own needs as a way God might be showing them something and/or an opportunity to move in a new direction. Again, as an opening devotion, a part of worship, or part of a meeting or educational event, ask these three questions:

> *What unfulfilled need do you have in your life right now?*

> *How could that need be filled if you turned to somebody in your life either to extend help to them or to receive it?*

> *What are the good things that might happen if you did that?*

Don't make them share their answers with you or the group if they don't want to. But do ask them to share what they've learned from this exercise. Help them see how their needs could actually be a good thing and an opportunity. If they can see that in their personal lives, they may be able to see it more easily in your shared life together.

Shine a light on it

If you did asset mapping (see page 100) using a wall, you provided a place where people could actually 'see the writing on the wall'—a visible reminder of all that you have to work with. Try collecting information about the Wows and Needs in your organization in a way that gives everybody access to the information so that together they can begin to get a sense of what God is doing and where God is directing you. Dedicate a bulletin board or a wall somewhere in your building to Wows and another one to Needs. Encourage people to write down on notecards the Wows they see in your life together and post them; have them do the same with the Needs they see. Find ways to help people talk about what they see emerging. Use the information that is being gathered in your own planning. Set people free to do what they hear God calling them to do as they respond to the needs they see and/or join in the amazing things God is already doing.

The third lens in the PAWN process helps keep your eyes open to what God is up to in and through your life together. It prevents you from getting tied in knots about what you think (or wish) you should be or have. It squashes "if-only" thinking by helping you see who you are and what you have that can make a difference in the world right here and right now. For real.

CONCLUSION
DISCOVERING NEW POSSIBILITIES FOR ACTION

"The PAWN process helps you discover what is and what is emerging in your context so that you can be useful to God."

A Washington, DC, area soup kitchen serves food to the many homeless and working poor people who live nearby. If you came to see it a few years ago, you would have seen what you see at many soup kitchens. Well meaning, well-to-do people would have been gathered in the kitchen cooking and serving food and talking to each other. Struggling hungry people would come through the line to get their food and then sit at tables in the cafeteria area to eat it. You would have had no trouble telling the 'haves' from the 'have-nots.' There was little mixing and no relationships being formed between the two groups.

But the people operating this particular soup kitchen dared to begin seeing their life and work together with new eyes. They were challenged by the idea that God is on the loose and at work in the world. They allowed themselves to recognize that everyone has assets, gifts and passions to contribute; even homeless and poor people have more than just needs. They started to imagine what two-directional ministry might look like, and they risked changing the ground rules they had inherited from generations of one-directional ministry.

The first change they made was to make sure that everyone who cooked and served in the kitchen also ate at the tables with the people who came for a meal. The regulars who ate there would be asked to participate in making the meal happen; some worked to set up tables, others helped prepare the food. This made it possible for people to get to know each other; they could talk about their gifts and passions; they could talk about the amazing things God was doing in their lives; they could talk about their needs. But they got serious about collecting this information, too.

One of the homeless women was asked to sit at a table near the door and talk to people as they came in. She was instructed to ask each person a few questions about what they liked to do and what they were good at. They were asked what they thought about the meals and the way the kitchen was operated and invited to give their suggestions. That's how they started making the shift to a new way of working together. It all began with seeing things, and each other, differently.

Today if you visit this soup kitchen, you will see a brand new community living and working together; that old one-directional ministry is long gone. Everybody eats together. Everybody cooks together. What happens in this ministry, and how it happens, is determined by the community—the whole community.

As is so often the case when people begin to see each other with new eyes, this ministry is no longer just about sharing food. Because they began to get to know each other, they uncovered gifts and passions right there in their midst that they never knew existed. Today, a jazz ensemble, composed of homeless and poor people as well as people who are financially well off, has chased away the somber mood you often find in such places.[11]

Could the people who ran this soup kitchen have predicted that they would form a jazz ensemble? No. Neither can they predict all of the other remarkable things that will emerge as they live and work together, paying attention to what God is doing in their midst and daring to join in.

What might happen in the place you live, work and serve if you dare to see things with new eyes?

---

[11] The basic outline of this story was shared with one of the members of our team by Jody Kretzmann, one of the pioneers of Asset-Based Community Development and a faculty member at Northwestern University.

EXPECT EMERGENCE

If you're anything like millions of other people around the world, you've seen the monster-hit *Avatar*, which has now become the highest grossing film of all time. Steven Spielberg called it "the most evocative and amazing science-fiction movie since *Star Wars*. [12] Using multiple projection cameras and polarized glasses, the creators of this film took a two-dimensional presentation and made it a three-dimensional experience.

That's what it should be like as you look around your world using the three PAWN lenses: God, neighbor, self. The PAWN process trains your eyes to pay attention to what is and what is emerging in your context so that you can be useful to God. As each lens overlaps, you begin to see old things in new ways and new things that you never saw before. That's why we have put an eye at the center of the diagram. Where the three lenses come together, you "discover" that all kinds of new things are possible. You see opportunities emerge when your neighbors' Assets, Wows and Needs are brought into focus with your own. Those opportunities and possibilities are represented by the fourth arrow (actually a whole bunch of arrows) emerging from the center of the PAWN process diagram. But it is hard to convey on paper just how dynamic and multi-dimensional this way of seeing really is.

We have had to portray the PAWN process using a 2-D illustration. But what we're talking about is more like the experience of a 3-D movie. To fully appreciate the dynamic nature of the PAWN process, wrestle with the following kinds of questions using the three lenses for perspective. These questions will help you discover new possibilities for action:

[12] HeatVision blog confirmed this in December 2009, before the movie was even released in theaters. http://www.heatvisionblog.com/2009/12/spielberg-on-avatar-the-most-evocative-scifi-movie-since-star-wars.html

What do you see God up to in the world around you?

Of the things you see God doing, which ones are most exciting to you and seem to invite you to just jump in?

Which good things already being done by your neighbors are most consistent with your sense of purpose and what God is calling your group to be about? Could you use any of your assets to help them?

What good things that God is already doing through you are most connected to the passions of your neighbors? Could you invite them to join you in them?

What needs do you have that could be met by resources already present in the neighbors around you? Are any of those relationships strong enough yet to ask for help? How could you proceed to explore or expand on this?

What wows are you involved in that overlap with Wows out in the community? Should you consider an alliance or partnership in some way?

What needs did you discover in your neighbors that your assets, gifts and passions could meet in a way that would make God smile?

What passions lie in your organization that you also found in some of your neighbors? Could God use you to work together to produce something that could become a new Wow?

What assets and gifts has God given you that could be useful to someone else? Are you open to encouraging people in your group to offer these to someone else?

Which things that you found that break God's heart most touch your heart? What could you, along with others you have met, do about them?

If you just skimmed through the list of questions go back and look at them again. Spend time really reflecting on them. Talk to others in your organization about them and encourage them to ask them, too. Together, you will discover all kinds of possibilities for action emerging as you allow what God is up to in your life to converge with what God is up to in your context. All of the possibilities that emerge when these three lenses—God, neighbor, self—converge are represented by the multiple arrows springing up from the center eye on the PAWN process diagram. So many possibilities begin to emerge, in fact, that it can be dizzying.

This is why it's important to have clarity about what's in your sense-making lens. Your purpose, principles and directions will help you figure out which possibilities to pursue. Go back to them again and again. Use them as a filter to rule out certain actions and to encourage others. Let them guide you.

It's also important to remember, as you make plans and take action, that you've decided to go with the flow. The PAWN process is not a tool (like the SWOT [Strengths, Weaknesses, Opportunities, Threats] Analysis, for example) that you use from time to time or turn on and off selectively. It is a way of seeing, experiencing and making sense of reality in order to see life more fully all the time. This way of seeing will become more natural over time and with practice.

Once you and the people in your organization are used to seeing this way all the time, you'll find that most of your planning will be very short-term. In fact, where you see possibilities to change things that are breaking God's heart or to accomplish something that will make God smile, you'll mostly work hard to not kill the chance by overplanning.

Instead of producing pictures of some idealized future and then trying to make it happen, you will watch for what God is already doing. You won't worry too much about making the 'right' decision or doing the most rational thing. As possibilities for action emerge, you'll just pick from the ones that are consistent with your purpose and that everybody seems to like the most. You'll go where the energy and the passion is. You'll do what seems right to you and to the Holy Spirit. You'll pitch in to help, right here and right now, and you'll dare to leave the results up to God. You will *do what matters*.